From Kitchen School to Learning Academy
Written by Barbara Nelson Bennet
Illustrated by Gabyriella Foster

This book is a work of nonfiction based on real events. Some names, details, and dialogues may have been adapted for storytelling purposes.

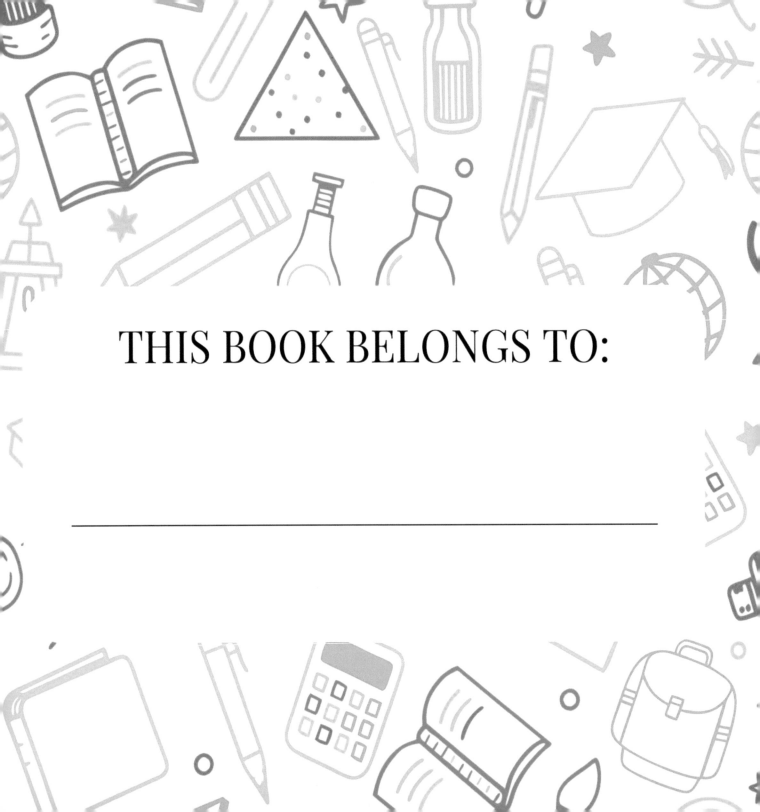

THIS BOOK BELONGS TO:

_____

Dedicated to Mrs. Dorothy M. Nelson, who had a dream and did not stop dreaming or praying. Your life has touched hundreds of children and made them the leaders of tomorrow.

Beyond the Kitchen

The Story of Bethlehem Junior Academy

Barbara Nelson Bennett

A long time ago, in a little kitchen, Mrs. Nelson had a big dream. She wanted to teach children everything they needed to know.

Mrs. Nelson was teaching Ashley how to read and one day, her mother approached Mrs. Dorothy and asked her if she could teach Ashley.

Mrs. Nelson beamed with excitement, smiled and said, "Of course!"

So, Mrs. Nelson taught Ashley right there in her kitchen. They read books, counted numbers, and learned about the world. Ashley was happy!

Soon, another child came. Then another. And another!

Mrs. Nelson's kitchen was full of laughter and learning.

But soon, there was no more room!
Where would the children learn now?

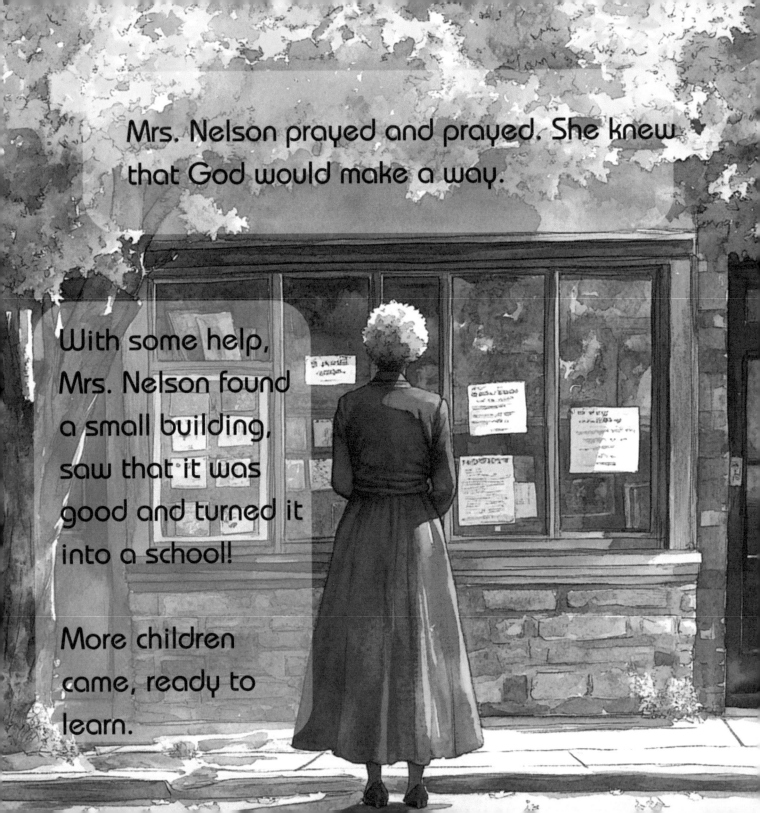

Mrs. Nelson prayed and prayed. She knew that God would make a way.

With some help, Mrs. Nelson found a small building, saw that it was good and turned it into a school!

More children came, ready to learn.

The little school grew and grew...
Until once again, there was no more room!

Mrs. Nelson never gave up. She had a dream and knew that teaching children was her passion. She continued to pray and trusted God.

She knew that she could not do it alone. She shared her dream with her family and her children. With their help, Mrs. Nelson's dream would come true.

With the help of others, Mrs. Nelson found a BIGGER place for her school.

Now, she has two buildings!

One for little learners in preschool and one for kindergarten through 8th grade!

What started in a small kitchen with one child...

 Became a big school with hundreds of students!

Mrs. Nelson's dream came true!

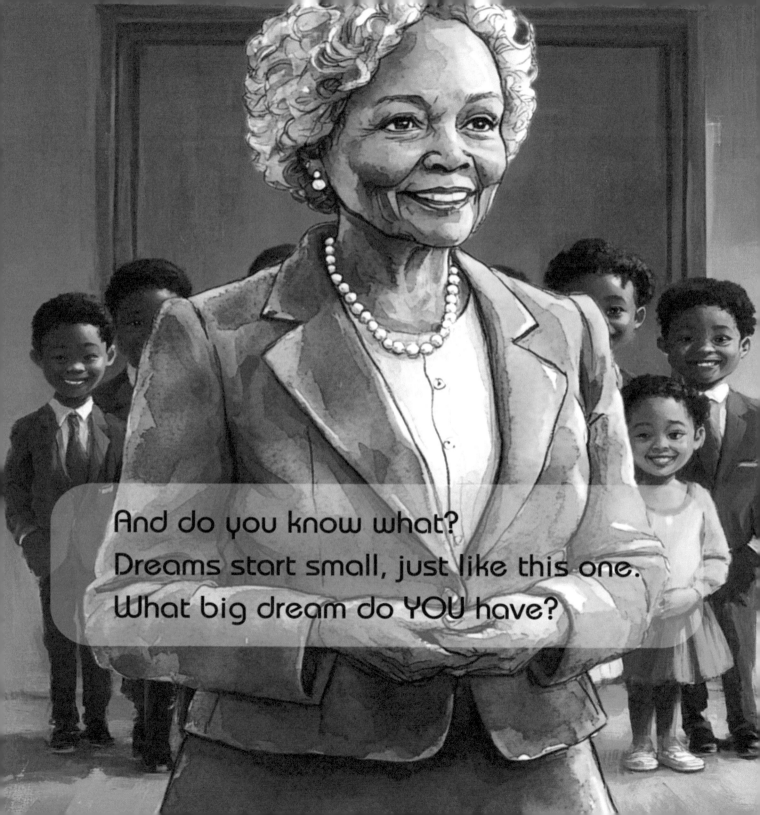

And do you know what?
Dreams start small, just like this one.
What big dream do YOU have?

Dorothy M. Nelson, a native of Jamaica, migrated to the United States in 1981 with her husband and three children. After working in Corporate America for several years, she transitioned to education, spending a year at a local preschool. Her passion for teaching and commitment to providing quality education for all children—regardless of color, class, or creed—led her to establish Bethlehem Preschool in her home, starting with just one student.

As enrollment grew, Dorothy, with the support of her daughter, moved the school into a larger facility that accommodated 50 students. Within a year, the demand for her high-quality early education program led to another expansion into a larger facility in North Lauderdale. Recognizing the advanced level of her preschool graduates, parents urged her to create a more challenging academic environment beyond preschool. This inspired her daughter, Audrey, to establish Bethlehem Junior Academy, K-8 institution dedicated to fostering excellence in education. On Saturday, May 14, 2024, they had the ribbon cutting for the newly purchased facility. The new facility has 20 classrooms, a library, cafeteria, computer room, and a multipurpose court that accommodates pickle ball, basketball and badminton!

Made in the USA
Columbia, SC
27 March 2025